SUCCESSFUL COOKING

HEARTY VEGETARIAN

INDEX

Contents

Vegetarian glossary

BLACK SESAME SEEDS: In their raw state, they have an earthy taste. If toasting, they need to be covered as they tend to pop.

BROAD (FAVA) BEANS: These thick-skinned beans have a nutty flavour and creamy texture. The tough outer skin is usually removed after cooking. They can be bought fresh or frozen – if fresh, remove the beans from the pods before cooking.

CASHEW PASTE: Roasted cashews are ground to form a paste. It is available from health-food stores and some supermarkets.

CASSIA BARK: This spice comes from the inner bark of a tropical evergreen tree. It is often mistaken for cinnamon and you can use cinnamon in its place.

CHILLI JAM: This sweet and sour jam is sold in jars at Asian food stores. Each brand varies in spiciness. For vegetarian cooking, make sure you read the label and choose one that doesn't contain shrimp paste.

CHINESE DRIED MUSHROOMS: Distinctly flavoured, this mixture of mushrooms needs to be soaked in boiling water for 10–15 minutes before use. Store them in a sealed container in a cool place.

CHOY SUM: This popular Chinese leaf vegetable has slightly bitter stems that are eaten more commonly than the leaves. Also known as flowering white cabbage.

COCONUT CREAM AND MILK: Both are extracted from the grated flesh of mature coconuts. The cream is a richer first pressing and the milk the second or third pressing. When a recipe uses cream, don't shake the can; use the thick cream on top.

COUSCOUS: This cereal is processed from semolina and coated with wheat flour. Instant couscous cooks in 5 minutes in boiling water.

DRIED RICE VERMICELLI: After soaking, these thin, translucent rice sticks develop a slippery texture and absorb the flavours of other food.

GHEE: A clarified unsalted butter used in Indian cooking. It has a higher burning point than other oils and fats.

GOW GEE WRAPPERS: These round wrappers are made from a wheat flour and water dough. They are usually used for steaming.

HALOUMI CHEESE: A soft semi-hard cheese with a salty flavour made from sheep's or goat's milk.

HARICOT BEANS: These small, white, oval beans have a bland flavour that absorbs other flavours well. Choose smooth-skinned beans with a creamy white colour.

JAPANESE SOY SAUCE: This is much lighter and sweeter than Chinese soy sauce. It is naturally brewed, so refrigerate after opening.

MAKRUT (KAFFIR) LIME LEAVES: Highly fragrant, these leaves are used in curries, salads and soups. The leaves can be frozen. Dried leaves need to be soaked in boiling water.

KECAP MANIS: Widely used in Indonesian and Malaysian cooking, this is a thick sweet soy sauce. If it's not available, use soy sauce sweetened with a little soft brown sugar.

KEFALOTYRI CHEESE: A very hard, scalded cured sheep's or goat's milk cheese with a milder flavour than Parmesan. Buy at delicatessens.

LENTILS: Packed with vitamins, there are many sizes, varieties and colours. Red, green and brown are the most common types. Green and brown lentils are often mixed together and can be substituted for each other. There's no need to soak lentils before cooking. They go mushy if cooked for too long.

MIRIN: A sweet rice wine with a low alcohol content, mirin is used extensively in Japanese cooking.

MISO: Fermented tofu and grains left to mature and gradually darken in colour. Shiro miso is a very light-coloured, almost sweet miso suitable for salad dressings.

NORI SHEETS: The most common form of dried seaweed. It comes plain or roasted (for a more palatable flavour). The paper-thin sheets are usually used as a wrapper for sushi.

PALM SUGAR: Available in blocks or in jars from Asian food stores. Soft brown sugar can be used instead.

PRESERVED LEMONS: A Moroccan speciality, quartered lemons are packed in a jar with salt and lemon juice, then refrigerated. Before use, rinse and discard the flesh and pith.

PUY LENTILS: These lentils are smaller and plumper than brown or green lentils. They are slate-coloured, have a peppery flavour and hold their shape well during cooking.

RICE-PAPER WRAPPERS: With a distinctive basket-weave pattern, these square or round thin sheets are bought dried and will keep indefinitely, but be careful – they are very brittle. Before using, briefly soak them one at a time in warm water so they become pliable.

RICE VINEGAR: Made from vinegar and a natural rice extract. Seasoned rice vinegar is similar but has sugar and salt added.

SAKE: A Japanese rice wine, sake is used as a drink and a cooking liquid.

SOBA NOODLES: Made from buckwheat flour, these noodles are usually available dried and sometimes fresh. They are eaten hot or cold.

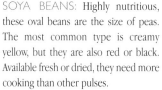

SOYA BEANS: Highly nutritious, these oval beans are the size of peas. The most common type is creamy yellow, but they are also red or black. Available fresh or dried, they need more cooking than other pulses.

TAHINI: A thick paste made from ground white sesame seeds and sesame oil. It has a bitter flavour.

TAMARI: Tamari is a naturally fermented dark soy sauce. Some varieties are wheat-free.

TEMPEH: Similar to tofu, tempeh is made from fermented soya beans. Quite firm in texture, it is suitable for most types of cooking.

TOFU

silken tofu: A very soft tofu often used in soups. Take care when cooking with it or it will break up.

silken firm tofu: Slightly firmer than silken tofu, it holds its shape a little better. Use in soups.

firm tofu: This soft tofu will hold its shape when cooking. It is suitable for stir-frying, pan-frying and baking.

hard tofu: Rubbery and firm, it won't break up during cooking. Use for stir-frying, pan-frying or as a base for patties.

tofu tempeh: Tofu and tempeh are combined and pressed together. Use in the same way as firm tofu.

fried tofu puffs: Tofu is aerated and then deep-fried. Use in stir-fries, curries and soups.

VEGETARIAN OYSTER SAUCE: This has a similar flavour to oyster sauce, but uses mushrooms as its flavour base.

WAKAME: A curly-leaf brown algae with a mild vegetable taste and soft texture. Dried wakame can be used in salads or as a vegetable after boiling. Use sparingly – its volume increases by about 10 times. You can use kombu or other seaweeds if necessary.

WASABI PASTE: From the edible root of a plant native to Japan. The skinned green root has a strong flavour like horseradish.

WON TON WRAPPERS: Thin squares made from wheat flour and egg yolks.

YELLOW SPLIT PEAS: A pea allowed to mature and dry on the vine. Normally dehusked and split. No soaking needed.

Items not available in the supermarket are available in specialist shops.

Poached Eggs with Garlic Yoghurt Dressing and Spinach

PREPARATION TIME: 10 minutes

TOTAL COOKING TIME: 15 minutes

SERVES 4

125 g (½ cup) sheep's milk yoghurt
1 small clove garlic, crushed
1 tablespoon snipped fresh chives
300 g (10½ oz) baby English spinach leaves,
  washed
30 g (1 oz) butter, chopped
herbed salt
4 tomatoes, halved
1 tablespoon white vinegar
8 eggs
1 round loaf light rye bread,
  cut into eight thick slices

1 To make the dressing, mix together the yoghurt, garlic and chives.

2 Wash the spinach and place it in a large saucepan with a little water clinging to the leaves. Cook, covered, over low heat for 3–4 minutes, or until wilted. Add the butter. Season with herbed salt. Set aside and keep warm. Cook the tomatoes under a hot grill for 3–5 minutes.

3 Fill a frying pan three-quarters full with cold water and add the vinegar and some salt to stop the egg whites spreading. Bring to a gentle simmer. Gently break the eggs one by one into a small bowl, carefully slide each one into the water, then reduce the heat so that the water barely moves. Cook for 1–2 minutes, or until the eggs are just set. Remove with an egg flip. Drain.

4 Toast the bread. Top each slice of toast with spinach, an egg and some dressing. Serve with tomato halves.

Cook spinach leaves until they are wilted, then stir in the butter.

Cook the eggs until they are just set, then remove with an egg flip.

Ricotta Pancakes with Goat's Milk Yoghurt and Pears

PREPARATION TIME: 15 minutes
TOTAL COOKING TIME: 50 minutes
SERVES 4

185 g (1½ cups) plain (all-purpose) flour
2 teaspoons baking powder
2 teaspoons ground ginger
2 tablespoons caster (superfine) sugar
4 eggs, separated
350 g (12 oz) low-fat ricotta
1 pear, peeled, cored and grated
315 ml (1¼ cups) milk
40 g (1½ oz) butter
3 beurre bosc pears, unpeeled
40 g (1½ oz) butter, extra
1 tablespoon soft brown sugar
1 teaspoon ground cinnamon
200 g (7 oz) goat's milk yoghurt

1 Sift the flour, baking powder, ginger and sugar into a bowl and make a well in the centre. Pour the combined egg yolks, ricotta, grated pear and milk into the well and mix until smooth.

2 Beat the egg whites until soft peaks form, then fold into the mixture.

3 Melt some butter in a frying pan over medium heat. Pour 60 ml (¼ cup) of the batter into the pan and swirl to create an even pancake. Cook for 1–1½ minutes, or until bubbles form, then turn and cook the other side for 1 minute, or until golden. Repeat with the remaining butter and mixture to make 11 more pancakes. Keep warm.

4 Cut the pears lengthways into thick slices. Melt the extra butter in a frying pan and stir in the sugar and cinnamon until the sugar dissolves. Cook the pears in batches, turning once, until tender. Serve stacks of pancakes with the pears and yoghurt.

Stir combined egg yolks, ricotta, pear and milk into the flour.

Cook the pancakes until bubbles form on the surface, then turn.

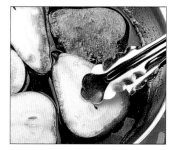

Cook pears in batches in buttery sauce, turning to coat in mixture.

Fried Tomatoes with Marinated Haloumi

PREPARATION TIME: 15 minutes +
overnight marinating
TOTAL COOKING TIME: 10 minutes
SERVES 4

400 g (14 oz) haloumi cheese, cut into eight
  1 cm (½ inch) slices
250 g (9 oz) cherry tomatoes, halved
250 g (9 oz) teardrop (pear) tomatoes,
  halved
1 clove garlic, crushed
2 tablespoons lemon juice
1 tablespoon balsamic vinegar
2 teaspoons fresh lemon thyme
60 ml (¼ cup) extra virgin olive oil
2 tablespoons olive oil
1 small loaf good-quality wholegrain bread,
  cut into eight thick slices

1 Place the haloumi and tomatoes in a non-metallic dish. Whisk together the garlic, lemon juice, vinegar, thyme and extra virgin olive oil and pour over the haloumi and tomatoes. Cover and marinate for 3 hours or overnight. Drain well, reserving the marinade.

2 Heat the olive oil in a large frying pan. Cook the haloumi in batches over medium heat for 1 minute each side, or until golden. Remove and keep warm. Add the tomatoes and cook over medium heat for 5 minutes, or until their skins begin to burst. Remove and keep warm.

3 Toast the bread until golden. Serve the haloumi on top of the toasted bread, piled high with the tomatoes and drizzled with the reserved marinade. Serve immediately.

Pour the marinade over the haloumi and mixed tomatoes.

Cook the haloumi until golden brown on both sides.

Cook the tomatoes until their skins start to burst.

13

Mixed Mushrooms in Brioche

PREPARATION TIME: 15 minutes
TOTAL COOKING TIME: 20 minutes
SERVES 6

750 g (1 lb 10 oz) mixed mushrooms (Swiss brown, shiitake, button, field, oyster)
75 g (2½ oz) butter
4 spring onions, chopped
2 cloves garlic, crushed
125 ml (½ cup) dry white wine
300 ml (10½ fl oz) carton cream
2 tablespoons chopped fresh thyme
6 small brioche

1 Preheat oven to moderate 180°C (350°F/Gas 4). Cut larger mushrooms into thick slices but leave the smaller ones whole.

2 Heat butter in a large frying pan over medium heat. Add spring onion and garlic and cook for 2 minutes. Increase heat, add mushrooms and cook, stirring frequently, for 5 minutes, or until the mushrooms are soft and all the liquid has evaporated. Pour in wine and boil for 2 minutes to reduce slightly.

3 Stir in cream and boil for a further 5 minutes to reduce and slightly thicken the sauce. Season to taste with salt and cracked black pepper. Stir in thyme and set aside for 5 minutes.

4 Slice tops off brioche and, using your fingers, pull out a quarter of the bread. Place brioche and their tops on baking tray and warm in oven for 5 minutes.

5 Place each brioche onto individual serving plates. Spoon mushroom sauce into each brioche, allowing it to spill over one side. Replace the top and serve warm.

Cut large mushrooms into thick slices; leave smaller ones whole.

Cook the mushrooms, stirring frequently, until they are soft.

Add the cream and cook until the sauce thickens slightly.

15

Baked Ricotta with Preserved Lemon and Semi-dried Tomatoes

PREPARATION TIME: 15 minutes +
10 minutes standing
TOTAL COOKING TIME: 30 minutes
SERVES 8–10

2 kg (4 lb 8 oz) wheel ricotta
olive oil spray
2 cloves garlic, crushed
1 preserved lemon, rinsed, pith and flesh
  removed, cut into thin strips
150 g (5½ oz) semi-dried (sun-blushed)
  tomatoes, roughly chopped
30 g (1 cup) finely chopped fresh flat-leaf
  parsley
50 g (1 cup) chopped fresh coriander
  (cilantro) leaves
80 ml (⅓ cup) extra virgin olive oil
60 ml (¼ cup) lemon juice

1 Preheat the oven to very hot 250°C (500°F/Gas 10). Place the ricotta on a baking tray lined with baking paper, spray lightly with the oil spray and bake for 20–30 minutes, or until golden brown. Stand for 10 minutes then, using egg flips, transfer to a large platter. (If possible, have someone help you move the ricotta.)

2 Meanwhile, place the garlic, preserved lemon, semi-dried tomato, parsley, coriander, oil and lemon juice in a bowl and mix together well.

3 Spoon the dressing over the baked ricotta, and serve with crusty bread.

Remove the flesh from the lemon and cut the rind into thin strips.

Mix all the dressing ingredients together in a bowl.

Spoon the dressing evenly over the baked ricotta.

Vegetable, Feta and Pesto Parcels

PREPARATION TIME: 40 minutes
TOTAL COOKING TIME: 30 minutes
SERVES 4

25 g (1 oz) butter
2 cloves garlic, crushed
155 g (5½ oz) asparagus spears, trimmed and cut into 2 cm (¾ inch) pieces
1 carrot, cut into julienne strips
1 zucchini (courgette), cut into julienne strips
1 red capsicum (pepper), cut into julienne strips
6 spring onions (scallions), thinly sliced on the diagonal
80 g (3 oz) mild feta cheese, crumbled
8 sheets filo pastry
60 g (2¼ oz) butter, melted
80 g (⅓ cup) good-quality ready-made pesto
2 teaspoons sesame seeds

1 Preheat the oven to moderately hot 200°C (400°F/Gas 6). Heat the butter in a large frying pan, then add the garlic and vegetables. Cook over medium heat for 3–4 minutes, or until just tender. Cool completely and fold in the feta. Divide the mixture into four equal portions.

2 Work with four sheets of pastry at a time, keeping the rest covered with a damp tea towel. Brush each sheet with melted butter and lay them on top of one another. Cut in half widthways and spread 1 tablespoon of the pesto in the centre of each half, leaving a 2 cm (¾ inch) border length-ways. Place one portion of the filling mixture on top of the pesto. Repeat with the remaining pastry, pesto and filling.

3 Brush the edges of filo with a little butter, tuck in the sides and fold over the ends to make four parcels. Place on a greased baking tray, seam-side-down, brush with the remaining butter and sprinkle with sesame seeds. Bake for 20–25 minutes, or until golden. Cut in half diagonally and serve hot with tomato chutney.

Cook garlic and vegetables over medium heat until just tender.

Cover the pesto with one portion of the vegetable feta mixture.

Tuck in sides and roll up parcel until it sits on the unsecured end.

Mediterranean Layered Cob

PREPARATION TIME: 45 minutes + 30 minutes
standing + overnight refrigeration
TOTAL COOKING TIME: 30 minutes
SERVES 6

2 eggplants (aubergines)
2 large red capsicums (peppers)
500 g (1 lb 2 oz) orange sweet potato, cut
  into thin slices
4 zucchini (courgettes), cut into
  1 cm (½ inch) slices lengthways
80 ml (⅓ cup) olive oil
23 cm (9 inch) round cob loaf
165 g (6 oz) good-quality ready-made pesto
200 g (7 oz) ricotta
35 g (⅓ cup) grated Parmesan

1 Cut eggplants lengthways into 1 cm (½ inch) slices and put in a colander. Sprinkle with salt and leave for 30 minutes, then rinse well.

2 Quarter capsicums and remove seeds and membranes. Cook under a hot grill (broiler), skin-side-up, until skin blisters and blackens. Let cool, then peel. Brush zucchini, eggplant and sweet potato with oil and chargrill or barbecue until browned.

3 Cut lid from the top of loaf. Remove the soft bread from inside, leaving a 1 cm (½ inch) shell. Brush inside and lid with pesto. Layer zucchini and capsicum inside the loaf, then spread with combined ricotta and Parmesan. Layer sweet potato and eggplant, lightly pressing down. Replace lid.

4 Cover loaf with plastic wrap and place on a baking tray. Put a tray on top of the loaf and weigh down with food cans. Refrigerate overnight.

5 Preheat the oven to very hot 250°C (500°F/Gas 10). Remove the plastic wrap, then bake for 10 minutes, or until crispy. Cut into wedges to serve.

Chargrill eggplant, sweet potato and zucchini until well browned.

Remove the soft bread from inside the loaf, leaving a shell.

Layer sweet potato and eggplant inside loaf over other ingredients.

Corn and Polenta Pancakes with Tomato Salsa

PREPARATION TIME: 15 minutes
TOTAL COOKING TIME: 10 minutes
SERVES 4

Tomato salsa
2 ripe tomatoes
150 g (1 cup) frozen broad (fava) beans
2 tablespoons chopped fresh basil
1 small Lebanese (short) cucumber, diced
2 small cloves garlic, crushed
1½ tablespoons balsamic vinegar
1 tablespoon extra virgin olive oil

Corn and polenta pancakes
90 g (¾ cup) self-raising flour
110 g (¾ cup) fine polenta
250 ml (1 cup) milk
310 g (10½ oz) can corn kernels, drained
olive oil, for pan-frying

1 Score a cross in the base of each tomato, then place in boiling water for 30 seconds. Plunge into cold water and peel the skin away from the cross. Dice. Pour boiling water over the broad beans and leave for 2–3 minutes. Drain and rinse. Remove the skins. Combine the beans, tomato, basil, cucumber, garlic, vinegar and oil.

2 To make the pancakes, sift the flour into a bowl and stir in the polenta. Add the milk and corn and stir until just combined, adding more milk if the mixture is too dry. Season.

3 Heat the oil in a frying pan and spoon half the mixture into the frying pan, making four 9 cm (3½ inch) pancakes. Cook for 2 minutes each side, or until golden and cooked through. Repeat with the remaining mixture, adding more oil if necessary. Drain. Serve with the salsa.

After blanching, peel the skin off the broad beans.

Stir the milk and corn kernels into the flour and polenta mixture.

Cook the pancakes for 2 minutes each side, or until golden brown.

Tamari Nut Mix

PREPARATION TIME: 5 minutes +
10 minutes standing
TOTAL COOKING TIME: 25 minutes
SERVES 10–12 (Makes 4 cups)

250 g (9 oz) mixed nuts (almonds, Brazil
  nuts, peanuts, walnuts)
125 g (4½ oz) pepitas
125 g (1 cup) sunflower seeds
125 g (¾ cup) cashew nuts
125 g (¾ cup) macadamia nuts
125 ml (½ cup) tamari

1 Preheat the oven to very slow 140°C (275°F/Gas 1).
Lightly grease two large baking trays.

2 Place the mixed nuts, pepitas, sunflower seeds,
cashew nuts and macadamia nuts in a large bowl.
Pour the tamari over the nuts and seeds and toss
together well, coating them evenly in the tamari.
Leave for 10 minutes.

3 Spread the nut and seed mixture evenly over
the prepared baking trays and bake for
20–25 minutes, or until dry roasted. Cool
completely and store in an airtight container
for up to 2 weeks. Serve as a snack.

*Stir the tamari through the nuts,
pepitas and sunflower seeds.*

*Spread nut mixture evenly over
two lightly greased baking trays.*

*Cook nut mixture in the oven for
20–25 minutes, until dry roasted.*

Eggplant and Coriander Tostadas

PREPARATION TIME: 20 minutes
TOTAL COOKING TIME: 30 minutes
SERVES 4

1 small eggplant (aubergine), cut into cubes
½ red capsicum (pepper), cut into cubes
½ red onion, cut into thin wedges
2 tablespoons olive oil
1 large clove garlic, crushed
1 small loaf wood-fired bread, cut into
 twelve 1.5 cm (⅝ inch) slices
1 small ripe tomato, halved
2 tablespoons chopped fresh mint
2 tablespoons chopped fresh coriander
 (cilantro) roots, stems and leaves
50 g (1¾ oz) slivered almonds, toasted

1 Preheat the oven to very hot 240°C (475°F/Gas 9). Place the eggplant, capsicum, onion and oil in a large bowl and mix until the vegetables are well coated in the oil. Spread the vegetables in a single layer in a large roasting tin. Bake for 15 minutes, then turn and bake for a further 10 minutes, or until tender. Transfer to a bowl, add the garlic and season.

2 Bake the bread on a baking tray for 4 minutes, or until crisp. Rub the cut side of the tomato onto one side of the bread slices, squeezing the tomato to extract as much liquid as possible, then finely chop the flesh. Add to the vegetables along with the herbs.

3 Spoon the vegetable mixture onto the tomato side of the bread and sprinkle with the almonds. Serve immediately.

Lay the vegetable mixture in a single layer in a large roasting

Place the vegetable mixture and garlic in a bowl and mix together.

Rub cut side of the tomato onto one side of each slice of bread.

27

Vegetable Frittata with Hummus and Black Olives

PREPARATION TIME: 35 minutes + cooling time
TOTAL COOKING TIME: 40 minutes
Makes 30 pieces

2 large red capsicums (peppers)
600 g (1 lb 5 oz) orange sweet potato, cut into 1 cm (½ inch) slices
60 ml (¼ cup) olive oil
2 leeks, finely sliced
2 cloves garlic, crushed
250 g (9 oz) zucchini (courgettes), thinly sliced
500 g (1 lb 2 oz) eggplant (aubergines), cut into 1 cm (½ inch) slices
8 eggs, lightly beaten
2 tablespoons finely chopped fresh basil
125 g (1¼ cups) grated Parmesan
20 g (7 oz) ready-made hummus
black olives, pitted and halved, to garnish

1 Cut capsicums into large pieces, removing seeds and membrane. Place, skin-side-up, under a hot grill (broiler) until the skin blackens and blisters. Cool in a plastic bag. Peel.

2 Cook the sweet potato in a saucepan of boiling water for 4–5 minutes, or until just tender. Drain.

3 Heat 1 tablespoon of the oil in a deep round 23 cm (9 inch) frying pan and stir leek and garlic over medium heat for 1 minute. Add zucchini and cook for 2 minutes, then remove from the pan.

4 Heat remaining oil and cook eggplant in batches for 2 minutes each side, or until golden. Line base of pan with half the eggplant, then leek. Cover with capsicum, remaining eggplant and sweet potato.

5 Combine eggs, basil, Parmesan and some pepper. Pour over vegetables. Cook on low for 15 minutes, until almost cooked. Place pan under a hot grill for 2–3 minutes, until golden and cooked. Cool, then invert onto a board. Trim and cut into 30 squares. Top with hummus and half an olive.

Lay roasted capsicum pieces over the leek and zucchini mixture.

Pour egg mixture over vegetables so that they are covered.

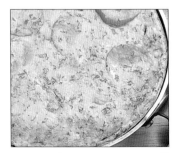
Cook the frittata under a hot grill until it is golden brown on top.

Tempura Vegetables with Wasabi Mayonnaise

PREPARATION TIME: 20 minutes
TOTAL COOKING TIME: 20 minutes
SERVES 4–6

Wasabi mayonnaise
2 tablespoons whole-egg mayonnaise
3 teaspoons wasabi paste
½ teaspoon grated lime rind

2 egg yolks
250 ml (1 cup) chilled soda water
30 g (¼ cup) cornflour (cornstarch)
110 g (4 oz) plain (all-purpose) flour
40 g (¼ cup) sesame seeds, toasted
oil, for deep-frying
1 small (250 g/9 oz) eggplant (aubergine), cut into thin rounds
1 large onion, cut into thin rounds, with rings intact
300 g (10½ oz) orange sweet potato, cut into thin rounds

1 To make wasabi mayonnaise, combine all ingredients in a bowl, cover with plastic wrap and refrigerate.

2 Place egg yolks and soda water in a jug and whisk lightly. Sift cornflour and flour into a bowl. Add sesame seeds and a good sprinkling of salt and mix well. Pour soda water and egg yolk mixture into the flour and stir lightly with chopsticks or a fork until just combined but still lumpy.

3 Fill a deep heavy-based saucepan or wok one-third full of oil and heat until a cube of bread dropped into the oil browns in 15 seconds. Dip pairs of the vegetables—eggplant and onion or eggplant and sweet potato—into the batter and cook in batches for 3–4 minutes, or until golden brown and cooked through. Drain on crumpled paper towels; season well. Keep warm, but do not cover or the tempura coating will go soggy.

4 Transfer the tempura to a warmed serving platter and serve immediately with the wasabi mayonnaise.

Gently stir combined soda water and egg yolk into flour mixture.

Dip assorted pairs of the vegetables into the batter.

Deep-fry the vegetables until golden brown and cooked through.

Tofu Pastries

PREPARATION TIME: 30 minutes +
4 hours refrigeration
TOTAL COOKING TIME: 20 minutes
SERVES 4

150 g (5½ oz) firm tofu
2 spring onions (scallions), chopped
3 teaspoons chopped fresh coriander
  (cilantro) leaves
½ teaspoon grated orange rind
2 teaspoons soy sauce
1 tablespoon sweet chilli sauce
2 teaspoons grated fresh ginger
1 teaspoon cornflour (cornstarch)
60 g (¼ cup) sugar
125 ml (½ cup) seasoned rice vinegar
1 small Lebanese (short) cucumber, finely
  diced
1 small red chilli, thinly sliced
1 spring onion (scallion), extra, thinly sliced
  on the diagonal
2 sheets ready-rolled puff pastry
1 egg, lightly beaten

1 Drain the tofu, then pat dry and cut into 1 cm
(½ inch) cubes.

2 Put the spring onion, coriander, rind, soy and chilli
sauces, ginger, cornflour and tofu in a bowl and
gently mix. Cover, then refrigerate for 3–4 hours.

3 Place the sugar and vinegar in a small saucepan
and stir over low heat until the sugar dissolves.
Remove from the heat and add the cucumber,
chilli and extra spring onion. Cool.

4 Preheat the oven to hot 220°C (425°F/Gas 7). Cut
each pastry sheet into four squares. Drain the
filling and divide into eight. Place one portion in
the centre of each square and brush the edges
with egg. Fold into a triangle and seal the edges
with a fork.

5 Put the triangles on two lined baking trays, brush
with egg and bake for 15 minutes. Serve with the
sauce.

*Gently mix the tofu and other
ingredients together in a bowl.*

*Remove saucepan from heat; add
spring onion, cucumber and chilli.*

*Fold pastry to enclose the filling,
then seal the edges with a fork.*

Individual Vegetable Terrines with a Spicy Tomato Sauce

PREPARATION TIME: 40 minutes
TOTAL COOKING TIME: 50 minutes
SERVES 4

125 ml (½ cup) oil
2 zucchini (courgettes), sliced on diagonal
500 g (1 lb 2 oz) eggplant (aubergines), sliced
1 small fennel bulb, sliced
1 red onion, sliced
300 g (10½ oz) ricotta
50 g (½ cup) grated Parmesan
1 tablespoon chopped fresh
  flat-leaf (Italian) parsley
1 tablespoon chopped fresh chives
1 red and 1 yellow capsicum (pepper),
  grilled (broiled), peeled, cut into large
  pieces

Spicy tomato sauce
1 tablespoon oil
1 onion, finely chopped
2 cloves garlic, crushed
1 red chilli, seeded and chopped

425 g (15 oz) can chopped tomatoes
2 tablespoons tomato paste (purée)

1 Heat 1 tablespoon oil in large frying pan. Cook vegetables in batches over high heat for 5 minutes. Drain separately on paper towels.

2 Preheat oven to moderate 200°C (400°F/Gas 6). Mix the cheeses and herbs together well. Season.

3 Lightly grease and line four 315 ml (1¼ cup) ramekins. Using half the eggplant, layer base of each dish. Continue layering with zucchini, capsicum, cheese mixture, fennel and onion. Cover with remaining eggplant and press down. Bake for 10–15 minutes. Leave for 5 minutes before turning out.

4 To make sauce, heat oil in a saucepan and cook onion and garlic for 2–3 minutes. Add chilli, tomato and tomato paste and simmer for 5 minutes, or until thick and pulpy. Purée in a food processor. Return to saucepan and keep warm. Spoon over the terrines.

Cook capsicums under a hot grill until blackened. Cut into pieces.

Layer fennel over cheese mixture, then add a layer of onion.

Simmer the tomato sauce for 5 minutes, or until thick and pulpy.

Onion Bhajis with Spicy Tomato Sauce

PREPARATION TIME: 30 minutes
TOTAL COOKING TIME: 35 minutes
Makes about 25

Spicy tomato sauce
2–3 red chillies, chopped
1 red capsicum (pepper), diced
425 g (15 oz) can chopped tomatoes
2 cloves garlic, finely chopped
2 tablespoons soft brown sugar
1½ tablespoons cider vinegar

125 g (1 cup) plain (all-purpose) flour
2 teaspoons baking powder
½ teaspoon chilli powder
½ teaspoon ground turmeric
1 teaspoon ground cumin
2 eggs, beaten
50 g (1 cup) chopped fresh coriander
 (cilantro) leaves
4 onions, very thinly sliced
oil, for deep-frying

1 Combine the sauce ingredients with 60 ml (¼ cup) water in a saucepan. Bring to the boil, then reduce the heat and simmer for 20 minutes, or until it thickens. Remove from the heat.

2 To make the bhajis, sift the flour, baking powder, spices and 1 teaspoon salt into a bowl and make a well in the centre. Gradually add the combined egg and 60 ml (¼ cup) water, whisking to make a smooth batter. Stir in the coriander and onion.

3 Fill a deep heavy-based saucepan one third full of oil and heat until a cube of bread dropped into the oil browns in 15 seconds. Cook dessertspoons of the mixture in the oil in batches for 90 seconds each side, or until golden. Drain. Serve with sauce.

Using a sharp knife, cut the onions into very thin slices.

Stir the coriander and onion into the batter.

Drop spoonfuls of batter into oil and cook in batches until golden.

Sweet Potato and Lentil Pastry Pouches

PREPARATION TIME: 45 minutes

TOTAL COOKING TIME: 55 minutes

Makes 32

2 tablespoons olive oil
1 large leek, finely chopped
2 cloves garlic, crushed
125 g (4½ oz) button mushrooms, chopped
2 teaspoons ground cumin
2 teaspoons ground coriander
95 g (½ cup) brown or green lentils
125 g (½ cup) red lentils
500 ml (2 cups) vegetable stock
300 g (10½ oz) sweet potato, diced
4 tablespoons finely chopped fresh
  coriander (cilantro) leaves
8 sheets ready-rolled puff pastry
1 egg, lightly beaten
½ leek, extra, cut into 5 mm (¼ inch) wide
  strips
200 g (7 oz) plain yoghurt
2 tablespoons grated Lebanese (short)
  cucumber
½ teaspoon soft brown sugar

1 Preheat oven to moderately 200°C (400°F/Gas 6). Heat oil in a saucepan over medium heat and cook leek for 2–3 minutes. Add garlic, mushrooms, cumin and ground coriander and cook for 1 minute, or until fragrant.

2 Add combined lentils and stock and bring to the boil. Reduce heat and simmer for 20–25 minutes, stirring occasionally. Add sweet potato in the last 5 minutes. Transfer to a bowl and stir in the coriander. Season to taste. Cool.

3 Cut the pastry sheets into four even squares. Place 1½ tablespoons of filling into the centre of each square and bring the edges together to form a pouch. Pinch together, then tie with string. Lightly brush the party with egg and place on lined baking trays. Bake for 20–25 minutes, or until the pastry is puffed and golden.

4 Soak the leek strips in boiling water for 30 seconds. Remove the string and re-tie with a piece of blanched leek. Mix the yoghurt, cucumber and sugar in a bowl. Serve with the pouches.

Transfer to a bowl and stir in the coriander leaves.

Put filling in centre of each square, form a pouch and tie with string.

Blanch strips of leek by soaking for 30 seconds in boiling water.

Vegetable and Tofu Kebabs

PREPARATION TIME: 40 minutes +
30 minutes marinating
TOTAL COOKING TIME: 30 minutes
SERVES 4

500 g (1 lb 2 oz) firm tofu, cut into 2 cm
 (¾ inch) cubes
1 red capsicum (pepper), cut into 2 cm
 (¾ inch) cubes
3 zucchini (courgettes), cut into 2 cm
 (¾ inch) lengths
4 small onions, cut into quarters
300 g (10½ oz) button mushrooms, cut into
 quarters
125 ml (½ cup) tamari
125 ml (½ cup) sesame oil
3 cm (1¼ inch) piece ginger, peeled and
 grated
175 g (½ cup) honey
1 tablespoon sesame oil, extra
1 small onion, finely chopped
1 clove garlic, crushed
2 teaspoons chilli paste
250 g (1 cup) smooth peanut butter
250 ml (1 cup) coconut milk
1 tablespoon soft brown sugar
1 tablespoon tamari, extra
1 tablespoon lemon juice
40 g (¼ cup) peanuts, roasted and chopped
40 g (¼ cup) sesame seeds, toasted

1 Preheat the oven to hot 220°C (425°F/Gas 7). Soak 12 bamboo skewers in water for 2 hours. Thread the tofu, capsicum, zucchini, onions and mushrooms alternately onto the skewers. Lay out in a large flat dish.

2 Combine the tamari, oil, ginger and honey in a non-metallic bowl. Pour over the kebabs. Leave for 30 minutes. Cook on a hot barbecue or chargrill, basting and turning, for 10–15 minutes, or until tender. Keep warm.

3 Heat the extra oil in a frying pan over medium heat and cook the onion, garlic and chilli paste for 1–2 minutes, or until the onion is soft. Reduce the heat and stir in the peanut butter, coconut milk, sugar, extra tamari and lemon juice. Bring to the boil, then reduce to a simmer for 10 minutes, or until just thick. Stir in the peanuts. If the sauce is too thick, add water.

4 Drizzle peanut sauce over the kebabs and sprinkle with sesame seeds.

Mushroom Moussaka

PREPARATION TIME: 20 minutes

TOTAL COOKING TIME: 1 hour

SERVES 4–6

1 (250 g/9 oz) eggplant (aubergine), cut into
  1 cm (½ inch) slices
1 large potato, cut into 1 cm (½ inch) slices
30 g (1 oz) butter
1 onion, finely chopped
2 cloves garlic, finely chopped
500 g (1 lb 2 oz) flat mushrooms, sliced
400 g (14 oz) can chopped tomatoes
½ teaspoon sugar
40 g (1½ oz) butter, extra
40 g (⅓ cup) plain (all-purpose) flour
500 ml (2 cups) milk
1 egg, lightly beaten
40 g (1½ oz) grated Parmesan

1 Preheat oven to hot 220°C (425°F/
Gas 7). Line a baking tray with foil
and brush with oil. Arrange eggplant
and potato in a single layer and
season. Bake for 20 minutes.

2 Melt the butter in a frying pan over medium heat.
Cook the onion, stirring for 3–4 minutes, or until
soft. Add the garlic and cook for 1 minute.
Increase the heat to high, add the mushrooms,
stirring for 2–3 minutes, or until soft. Add the
tomato, reduce the heat and simmer rapidly for
8 minutes, or until reduced. Stir in the sugar.

3 Melt the extra butter in a saucepan over low heat.
Add the flour and cook for 1 minute, or until pale
and foaming. Remove from the heat and gradually
stir in the milk. Return to the heat, stirring until it
boils and thickens. Reduce the heat and simmer
for 2 minutes. Remove from the heat and, when
the bubbles subside, stir in the egg and Parmesan.

4 Reduce the oven to moderate 180°C (350°F/Gas 4).
Grease a shallow 1.5 litre (6 cup) ovenproof dish.
Spoon one third of the mushroom mixture into the
dish. Cover with the potato, half the remaining
mushrooms, then the eggplant. Finish with the
remaining mushrooms, pour on the sauce and
smooth the top. Bake for 30–35 minutes, or until
the edges bubble. Rest for 10 minutes and serve.

Stir the sugar into the thickened
vegetable mixture.

Remove saucepan from heat and
stir in the egg and Parmesan.

Cover the mushroom mixture
with the potato slices.

Tofu Burgers

PREPARATION TIME: 25 minutes +
30 minutes refrigeration
TOTAL COOKING TIME: 30 minutes
SERVES 6

1 tablespoon olive oil
1 red onion, finely chopped
200 g (7 oz) Swiss brown mushrooms, finely
  chopped
350 g (12 oz) hard tofu
2 large cloves garlic
3 tablespoons finely chopped fresh basil
200 g (2 cups) dry wholemeal breadcrumbs
1 egg, lightly beaten
2 tablespoons balsamic vinegar
2 tablespoons sweet chilli sauce
150 g (1½ cups) dry wholemeal breadcrumbs
olive oil, for shallow-frying
6 wholemeal or wholegrain bread rolls
125 g (½ cup) whole-egg mayonnaise
100 g (3½ oz) semi-dried (sun-blushed)
  tomatoes
60 g (2¼ oz) rocket (arugula)
sweet chilli sauce, to serve (optional)

1 Heat oil in a frying pan and cook onion over medium heat for 2–3 minutes. Add mushrooms and cook for a further 2 minutes. Cool slightly.

2 Blend 250 g (9 oz) of the tofu with garlic and basil in a food processor until smooth. Transfer to a large bowl and stir in onion mixture, breadcrumbs, egg, vinegar and sweet chilli sauce. Grate remaining tofu and fold through mixture, then refrigerate for 30 minutes. Form mixture into six patties, pressing together. Coat in breadcrumbs.

3 Heat 1 cm (½ inch) oil in a deep frying pan and cook the patties in two batches for 4–5 minutes each side, or until golden. Turn them over carefully to prevent them breaking up. Drain on crumpled paper towels and season.

4 Toast the bread rolls under a hot grill (broiler). To assemble, spread the mayonnaise over both sides of each toasted bread roll. On the bottom half of each roll, layer semi-dried tomatoes, a tofu patty and rocket leaves. Drizzle with sweet chilli sauce and top with the other half of the bread roll.

Blend the tofu, garlic and basil in a food processor until smooth.

Grate the remaining tofu and fold it into the mixture.

Carefully turn over the tofu patties with an egg flip.

45

Udon Noodle Stir-fry

PREPARATION TIME: 15 minutes
TOTAL COOKING TIME: 10 minutes
SERVES 4

500 g (1 lb 2 oz) fresh udon noodles
1 tablespoon oil
6 spring onions (scallions), cut into 5 cm
  (2 inch) lengths
3 cloves garlic, crushed
1 tablespoon grated fresh ginger
2 carrots, cut into 5 cm (2 inch) lengths
150 g (5½ oz) snow peas (mangetout), cut in
  half on the diagonal
100 g (3½ oz) bean sprouts
500 g (1 lb 2 oz) choy sum, cut into 5 cm
  (2 inch) lengths
2 tablespoons Japanese soy sauce
2 tablespoons mirin
2 tablespoons kecap manis
2 sheets roasted nori, cut into thin strips

1 Add the noodles to a pan of boiling water and cook for 5 minutes, or until tender. Drain and rinse under hot water.

2 Heat the oil in a wok until hot, then add the spring onion, garlic and ginger. Stir-fry over high heat for 1–2 minutes, or until soft. Add the carrot, snow peas and 1 tablespoon water, toss well, cover and cook for 1–2 minutes, or until just tender.

3 Add the noodles, bean sprouts, choy sum, soy sauce, mirin and kecap manis, then toss until the choy sum is wilted and coated with the sauce. Stir in the nori just before serving.

Cut the roasted nori sheets into very thin strips.

Cook udon noodles until tender and not clumped together.

Stir-fry the greens, noodles and sauces until well mixed.

Roast Sweet Potato Ravioli

PREPARATION TIME: 45 minutes
TOTAL COOKING TIME: 1 hour 10 minutes
SERVES 6

500 g (1 lb 2 oz) orange sweet potato,
  cut into large pieces
60 ml (¼ cup) olive oil
150 g (5½ oz) ricotta
1 tablespoon chopped fresh basil
1 clove garlic, crushed
2 tablespoons grated Parmesan
2 x 250 g (9 oz) packets egg won ton
  wrappers
50 g (1¾ oz) butter
4 spring onions (scallions), sliced on the
  diagonal
2 cloves garlic, crushed, extra
300 ml (10½ fl oz) carton cream
baby basil leaves, to serve

1 Preheat oven to hot 220°C
(425°F/Gas 7). Place sweet potato
on baking tray and drizzle with oil.
Bake for 40 minutes, until tender.

2 Transfer the sweet potato to a bowl with the ricotta,
basil, garlic and Parmesan and mash until smooth.

3 Cover the won ton wrappers with a damp tea
towel. Place 2 level teaspoons of the sweet potato
mixture into the centre of one wrapper and brush
the edges with a little water. Top with another
wrapper. Place onto a baking tray lined with baking
paper and cover with a tea towel. Repeat with the
remaining ingredients to make 60 ravioli, placing a
sheet of baking paper between each layer.

4 Melt the butter in a frying pan. Add the spring
onion and garlic and cook over medium heat for
1 minute. Add the cream, bring to the boil, then
reduce the heat and simmer for 4–5 minutes, or
until the cream has reduced and thickened. Keep
warm.

5 Bring a large saucepan of water to the boil. Cook
the ravioli in batches for 2–4 minutes, or until just
tender. Drain, then divide among serving plates.
Ladle the hot sauce over the top, garnish with
basil leaves and serve immediately.

*Drizzle the sweet potato with oil
and bake until golden.*

*Cover the filling with the won
ton wrapper.*

*Simmer the cream mixture until it
has reduced and thickened.*

Warm Pesto Pasta Salad

PREPARATION TIME: 20 minutes
TOTAL COOKING TIME: 20 minutes
SERVES 4

Pesto
2 cloves garlic, crushed
1 teaspoon sea salt
40 g (¼ cup) pine nuts, toasted
60 g (2 cups) fresh basil
50 g (½ cup) grated Parmesan
80 ml (⅓ cup) extra virgin olive oil

500 g (1 lb 2 oz) orecchiette or shell pasta
2 tablespoons olive oil
150 g (5½ oz) jar capers, drained and dried
2 tablespoons extra virgin olive oil
2 cloves garlic, chopped
3 tomatoes, seeded and diced
300 g (10½ oz) thin asparagus spears, halved
   and blanched
2 tablespoons balsamic vinegar
200 g (7 oz) rocket (arugula), cut into 3 cm
   (1¼ inch) lengths
shaved Parmesan, to garnish

1 To make pesto, place garlic, sea salt and pine nuts in a food processor or blender and process until combined. Add basil and Parmesan and process until finely minced. With the motor running, add oil in a thin steady stream and blend until smooth.

2 Cook the pasta in a large saucepan of boiling water until al dente, then drain well.

3 Meanwhile, heat oil in a frying pan, add capers and fry over high heat, stirring occasionally, for 4–5 minutes, or until crisp. Remove from the pan and drain on crumpled paper towels.

4 In the same frying pan, heat olive oil over medium heat and add the garlic, tomato and asparagus. Cook for 1–2 minutes, or until warmed through, tossing continuously. Stir in the balsamic vinegar.

5 Drain pasta and transfer to a large serving bowl. Add pesto and toss, coating pasta well. Cool slightly. Add tomato mixture and rocket and season to taste with salt and black pepper. Toss well and sprinkle with capers and Parmesan.

Fry the capers over high heat, stirring occasionally, until crisp.

Add the pesto and toss thoroughly through the pasta.

Chunky Chickpea and Herb Dumpling Soup

PREPARATION TIME: 30 minutes
TOTAL COOKING TIME: 35 minutes
SERVES 4

1 tablespoon oil
1 onion, chopped
2 cloves garlic, crushed
2 teaspoons ground cumin
1 teaspoon ground coriander
¼ teaspoon chilli powder
2 x 300 g (10½ oz) cans chickpeas, drained
875 ml (3½ cups) vegetable stock
2 x 425 g (15 oz) cans chopped tomatoes
1 tablespoon chopped fresh coriander
  (cilantro) leaves
125 g (1 cup) self-raising flour
25 g (1 oz) butter, chopped
2 tablespoons grated Parmesan
2 tablespoons mixed chopped fresh herbs
  (flat-leaf (Italian) parsley, coriander
  (cilantro) leaves and chives)
60 ml (¼ cup) milk

1 Heat the oil in a saucepan, and cook the onion over medium heat for 2–3 minutes, or until soft. Add the garlic, cumin, ground coriander and chilli and cook for 1 minute, or until fragrant. Add the chickpeas, stock and tomato. Bring to the boil, then reduce the heat and simmer, covered, for 10 minutes. Stir in the coriander.

2 To make the dumplings, sift the flour into a bowl and add the chopped butter. Rub the butter into the flour with your fingertips until it resembles fine breadcrumbs. Stir in the cheese and mixed fresh herbs. Make a well in the centre, add the milk and mix with a flat-bladed knife until just combined. Bring together into a ball, divide into eight portions and roll into small balls.

3 Add the dumplings to the soup, cover and simmer for 20 minutes, or until a skewer comes out clean when inserted in the centre of the dumplings.

Stir the coriander into the simmering chickpea mixture.

Add milk to dumpling mixture and mix with a flat-bladed knife.

Pierce the dumplings with a skewer to test if they are cooked.

Couscous Vegetable Loaf

PREPARATION TIME: 20 minutes + cooling time + overnight refrigeration
TOTAL COOKING TIME: 10 minutes
SERVES 6

1 litre (4 cups) vegetable stock
500 g (1 lb 2 oz) instant couscous
30 g (1 oz) butter
3 tablespoons olive oil
2 cloves garlic, crushed
1 onion, finely chopped
1 tablespoon ground coriander
1 teaspoon ground cinnamon
1 teaspoon garam masala
250 g (9 oz) cherry tomatoes, quartered
1 zucchini (courgette), diced
130 g (4½ oz) can corn kernels, drained
8 large fresh basil leaves
150 g (5½ oz) sun-dried (sun-blushed)
   capsicums (peppers) in oil
60 g (1 cup) chopped fresh basil, extra
80 ml (⅓ cup) orange juice
3 tablespoons chopped fresh flat-leaf
   (Italian) parsley

1 tablespoon lemon juice
1 teaspoon honey
1 teaspoon ground cumin

1 Bring stock to the boil. Put couscous and butter in a bowl, cover with stock. Leave for 10 minutes.

2 Heat 1 tablespoon of oil in a frying pan and cook garlic and onion over low heat for 5 minutes. Add spices and cook for 1 minute. Remove from pan.

3 Add remaining oil to the pan and cook tomatoes, zucchini and corn over high heat until soft.

4 Line a 3 litre (12 cup) loaf tin with plastic wrap, overhanging the sides. Form the basil into two flowers on the base. Drain capsicums, reserving 2 tablespoons of oil, then roughly chop. Add onion mix, tomato mix, capsicum and extra basil to couscous and mix. Cool.

5 Press the mixture into the tin and cover with the plastic wrap. Weigh down with cans and chill overnight.

6 Place the remaining ingredients and reserved capsicum oil in a jar with a lid and shake. Turn out the loaf, slice and serve with the dressing.

Arrange basil leaves in shape of two flowers in base of loaf tin.

Mix onion mixture, vegetables, capsicum, basil and couscous.

Green Curry with Sweet Potato and Eggplant

PREPARATION TIME: 15 minutes
TOTAL COOKING TIME: 25 minutes
SERVES 4–6

1 tablespoon oil
1 onion, chopped
1–2 tablespoons green curry paste
1 eggplant (aubergine), quartered and
  sliced
375 ml (1½ cups) coconut milk
250 ml (1 cup) vegetable stock
6 makrut (kaffir) lime leaves
1 orange sweet potato, cut into cubes
2 teaspoons soft brown sugar
2 tablespoons lime juice
2 teaspoons lime rind

1 Heat the oil in a large wok or frying pan. Add the onion and curry paste and cook, stirring, over medium heat for 3 minutes. Add the eggplant and cook for a further 4–5 minutes, or until softened. Pour in the coconut milk and stock, bring to the boil, then reduce the heat and simmer for 5 minutes. Add the lime leaves and sweet potato and cook, stirring occasionally, for 10 minutes, or until the vegetables are very tender.

2 Mix in the sugar, lime juice and lime rind until well combined with the vegetables. Season to taste with salt. Garnish with some fresh coriander leaves and extra lime leaves if desired, and serve with steamed rice.

Using a sharp knife, quarter and slice the eggplant.

Stir-fry the onion and curry paste over medium heat for 3 minutes.

Cook, stirring occasionally, until the vegetables are tender.

Mushroom Nut Roast with Tomato Sauce

PREPARATION TIME: 25 minutes
TOTAL COOKING TIME: 50 minutes
SERVES 6

2 tablespoons olive oil
1 large onion, diced
2 cloves garlic, crushed
300 g (10½ oz) cap mushrooms, finely
  chopped
200 g (1¼ cups) cashew nuts
200 g (1¼ cups) Brazil nuts
125 g (1 cup) grated Cheddar
25 g (¼ cup) grated Parmesan
1 egg, lightly beaten
2 tablespoons chopped fresh chives
80 g (1 cup) fresh wholemeal breadcrumbs
1½ tablespoons olive oil, extra
1 onion, finely chopped, extra
1 clove garlic, crushed, extra
400 g (14 oz) can chopped tomatoes
1 tablespoon tomato paste (purée)
1 teaspoon caster (superfine) sugar

1 Preheat the oven to moderate 180°C (350°F/Gas 4). Grease a 14 x 21 cm (5½ x 8½ inch) tin and line with baking paper. Heat the oil in a frying pan and fry the onion, garlic and mushrooms over medium heat for 2–3 minutes, or until soft. Cool.

2 Finely chop the nuts in a food processor, but do not over-process.

3 chives and breadcrumbs. Bake in the tin for 45 minutes, or until firm. Stand for 5 minutes, then turn out.

4 Heat the extra oil in a frying pan and add the extra onion and garlic. Cook over low heat for 5 minutes, or until soft. Add the tomato, paste, sugar and 80 ml (⅓ cup) water. Simmer for 3–5 minutes, or until thick.

Finely chop the cashews and Brazil nuts in a food processor.

Press the nutty mushroom mixture into the prepared tin.

Simmer the tomato mixture until thickened.

Vegetable Tart with Salsa Verde

PREPARATION TIME: 30 minutes +
30 minutes refrigeration
TOTAL COOKING TIME: 50 minutes
SERVES 6

215 g (1¾ cups) plain (all-purpose) flour
120 g (4 oz) chilled butter, cubed
60 ml (¼ cup) cream
1–2 tablespoons chilled water
1 (250 g/9 oz) Desirée potato, cut into 2 cm
  (¾ inch) cubes
1 tablespoon olive oil
2 cloves garlic, crushed
1 red capsicum (pepper), cut into cubes
1 red onion, sliced into rings
2 zucchini (courgettes), sliced
2 tablespoons chopped fresh dill
1 tablespoon chopped fresh thyme
1 tablespoon drained baby capers
150 g (5½ oz) marinated quartered arti-
  choke hearts, drained
30 g (⅔ cup) baby English spinach leaves

Salsa verde
1 clove garlic
40 g (2 cups) fresh flat-leaf (Italian) parsley
80 ml (⅓ cup) extra virgin olive oil
3 tablespoons chopped fresh dill
1½ tablespoons Dijon mustard
1 tablespoon red wine vinegar
1 tablespoon drained baby capers

1 Sift the flour and ½ teaspoon salt into a large
bowl. Add the butter and rub into the flour with
your fingertips until it resembles fine breadcrumbs.
Add the cream and water and mix with a flat-
bladed knife until the mixture comes together in
beads. Gather together and lift onto a lightly
floured work surface. Press into a ball, then flatten
into a disc, wrap in plastic wrap and refrigerate
for 30 minutes.

2 Preheat the oven to moderately hot 200°C
(400°F/Gas 6). Grease a 27 cm (10¾ inch) loose-
bottomed flan tin. Roll the dough out between
2 sheets of baking paper large enough to line the
tin. Remove the paper and invert the pastry into

*Mix with a flat-bladed knife until
mixture comes together in beads.*

*Remove paper and use a rolling
pin to invert pastry into the tin.*

*Bake the pastry case until it is dry
and golden brown.*

the tin. Use a small pastry ball to press the pastry into the tin, allowing any excess to hang over the side. Roll a rolling pin over the tin, cutting off any excess. Cover the pastry with a piece of crumpled baking paper, then add baking beads. Place the tin on a baking tray and bake for 15–20 minutes. Remove the paper and beads, reduce the heat to moderate 180°C (350°F/Gas 4) and bake for 20 minutes, or until golden.

3 To make the salsa verde, combine all the ingredients in a food processor and process until almost smooth.

4 Boil the potato until just tender. Drain. Heat the oil in a frying pan and cook the garlic, capsicum and onion over medium heat for 3 minutes, stirring often. Add the zucchini, dill, thyme and capers, cook for 3 minutes. Reduce the heat to low; add the potato and artichokes until heated. Season.

5 To assemble, spread 60 ml (¼ cup) of the salsa over the pastry. Spoon the vegetable mixture into the case and drizzle with half the remaining salsa. Pile the spinach in the centre and drizzle with the remaining salsa.

Cook vegetables until potato and artichokes are heated through.

Spread a little of the salsa verde over the pastry base.

Lay the spinach leaves in the centre of the vegetable mixture.

Spicy Vegetable Stew with Dhal

PREPARATION TIME: 25 minutes +
2 hours soaking
TOTAL COOKING TIME: 1 hour 35 minutes
SERVES 4–6

Dhal
165 g (¾ cup) yellow split peas
5 cm (2 inch) piece ginger, grated
2–3 cloves garlic, crushed
1 red chilli, seeded and chopped

3 tomatoes
2 tablespoons oil
1 teaspoon yellow mustard seeds
1 teaspoon cumin seeds
1 teaspoon ground cumin
½ teaspoon garam masala
1 red onion, cut into thin wedges
3 slender eggplants (aubergines), cut into
  2 cm (¾ inch) slices
2 carrots, cut into 2 cm (¾ inch) slices
¼ cauliflower, cut into florets
375 ml (1½ cups) vegetable stock
2 small zucchini (courgettes), cut into 3 cm
  (1¼ inch) slices

80 g (½ cup) frozen peas
15 g (½ cup) fresh coriander (cilantro) leaves

1 To make dhal, place split peas in a bowl, cover
with water and soak for 2 hours. Drain. Place in a
large saucepan with ginger, garlic, chilli and 750
ml (3 cups) water. Bring to the boil, then reduce
the heat and simmer for 45 minutes, or until soft.

2 Score a cross in base of tomatoes, soak in boiling
water for 2 minutes, then plunge into cold water
and peel skin away from cross. Remove seeds and
chop.

3 Heat oil in a large saucepan. Cook spices over
medium heat for 30 seconds, until fragrant. Add
onion and cook a further 2 minutes, until soft. Stir
in the tomato, eggplant, carrot and cauliflower.

4 Stir in dhal purée and stock and simmer, covered,
for 45 minutes, or until the vegetables are tender.
Stir often. Add the zucchini and peas during the
last 10 minutes of cooking. Stir in the coriander
and serve hot.

*Peel the skin away from the cross,
then remove the seeds and chop.*

*Simmer the dhal mixture until the
split peas are soft.*

*Simmer for 45 minutes, or until
the vegetables are tender.*

Fennel Risotto Balls with Cheesy Filling

PREPARATION TIME: 30 minutes +
1 hour refrigeration
TOTAL COOKING TIME: 50 minutes
SERVES 4–6

1.5 litres (6 cups) vegetable stock
1 tablespoon oil
30 g (1 oz) butter
2 cloves garlic, crushed
1 onion, finely chopped
2 fennel bulbs, finely sliced
1 tablespoon balsamic vinegar
125 ml (½ cup) white wine
660 g (3 cups) arborio rice
50 g (½ cup) grated Parmesan
25 g (½ cup) snipped fresh chives
1 egg, lightly beaten
150 g (5½ oz) sun-dried (sun-blushed) tomatoes, chopped
100 g (3½ oz) mozzarella, diced
80 g (½ cup) frozen peas, thawed
flour, for dusting
3 eggs, lightly beaten, extra
200 g (2 cups) dry breadcrumbs
oil, for deep-frying

1 Heat the stock in a saucepan, cover
and keep at a low simmer.

2 Heat oil and butter in a saucepan
and cook garlic and onion over
medium heat for 3 minutes. Add
fennel and cook for 10 minutes.

Add vinegar and wine, increase heat and boil until
liquid evaporates. Add rice and stir for 1 minute,
until translucent.

3 Add ½ cup (125 ml) hot stock, stirring constantly
over medium heat until the liquid is absorbed.
Continue adding more stock, ½ cup (125 ml) at a
time, stirring for 20–25 minutes, or until all stock
is absorbed and the rice is tender and creamy. Stir
in Parmesan, chives, egg and tomato. Transfer to
a bowl, cover and cool.

4 Place the mozzarella and peas in a bowl and mash
together. Season.

5 With wet hands, shape risotto into 14 even balls.
Flatten each ball out, slightly indenting centre.
Place a heaped teaspoon of the pea mash into the
indentation, then shape the rice around the filling
to form a ball. Roll each ball in seasoned flour,
then dip in the extra egg and roll in breadcrumbs.
Place on a foil-covered tray and refrigerate for
30 minutes.

6 Fill a deep heavy-based saucepan one third full of
oil and heat until a cube of bread dropped into
the oil browns in 15 seconds. Cook the risotto
balls in batches for 5 minutes, or until golden and
crisp and the cheese has melted inside. Drain on
crumpled paper towels and season with salt. If the
cheese has not melted, cook the balls on a tray in
a moderate 180°C (350°F/Gas 4) oven for
5 minutes. Serve with a salad or vegetables.

Pumpkin, Basil and Ricotta Lasagne

PREPARATION TIME: 20 minutes
TOTAL COOKING TIME: 1 hour 25 minutes
SERVES 4

650 g (1 lb 7 oz) pumpkin
2 tablespoons olive oil
500 g (1 lb 2 oz) ricotta
50 g (⅓ cup) pine nuts, toasted
35 g (¾ cup) firmly packed fresh basil
2 cloves garlic, crushed
35 g (⅓ cup) finely grated Parmesan
125 g (4½ oz) fresh lasagne sheets
185 g (1¼ cups) grated mozzarella

1 Preheat the oven to moderate 180°C (350°F/Gas 4). Lightly grease a baking tray. Cut the pumpkin into 1 cm (½ inch) slices and arrange in a single layer on the tray. Brush with oil and cook for 1 hour, or until softened, turning halfway through cooking.

2 Combine the ricotta, pine nuts, basil, garlic and Parmesan.

3 Brush a square 20 cm (8 inch) ovenproof dish with oil. Cook the pasta according to the packet instructions. Arrange one third of the pasta sheets over the base of the dish. Spread with the ricotta mixture. Top with half of the remaining lasagne.

4 Arrange the pumpkin evenly over the pasta with as few gaps as possible. Season and top with the final layer of pasta sheets. Sprinkle with mozzarella. Bake for 20–25 minutes, or until the cheese is golden. Leave for 10 minutes, then cut into squares.

Mix together the ricotta, pine nuts, basil, garlic and Parmesan.

Cook the pasta according to the packet instructions until al dente.

Place pumpkin pieces closely together on top of lasagne sheet.

Soya Bean Moussaka

PREPARATION TIME: 25 minutes

TOTAL COOKING TIME: 1 hour

SERVES 4

2 eggplants (aubergines)
1 tablespoon oil
1 onion, finely chopped
2 cloves garlic, crushed
2 ripe tomatoes, peeled, seeded and
   chopped
2 teaspoons tomato paste (purée)
½ teaspoon dried oregano
125 ml (½ cup) dry white wine
300 g (10½ oz) can soya beans, rinsed and
   drained
3 tablespoons chopped fresh flat-leaf
   (Italian) parsley
30 g (1 oz) butter
2 tablespoons plain (all-purpose) flour
pinch ground nutmeg
315 ml (1¼ cups) milk
40 g (⅓ cup) grated Cheddar

1 Preheat the oven to moderate 180°C (350°F/Gas 4). Cut the eggplants in half lengthways. Spoon out the flesh, leaving a 1.5 cm (⅝ inch) border and place on a large baking tray, cut-side-up. Use crumpled foil around the sides of the eggplant to help support it.

2 Heat the oil in a frying pan. Cook the onion and garlic over medium heat for 3 minutes, or until soft. Add the tomato, paste, oregano and wine. Boil for 3 minutes, or until the liquid is reduced and the tomato is soft. Stir in the soya beans and parsley.

3 To make the sauce, melt the butter in a saucepan. Stir in the flour and cook over medium heat for 1 minute, or until pale and foamy. Remove from the heat and gradually stir in the nutmeg and milk. Return to the heat and stir constantly until the sauce boils and thickens. Pour one third of the white sauce into the tomato mixture and stir well.

4 Spoon the mixture into the eggplant shells. Smooth the surface before spreading the remaining sauce evenly over the top and sprinkling with cheese. Bake for 50 minutes, or until cooked through. Serve hot. Serve with a fresh salad, if desired.

Scoop out eggplant flesh, leaving a border all the way around.

Add soya beans and parsley to the tomato mixture and stir well.

Vegetable Casserole with Herb Dumplings

PREPARATION TIME: 30 minutes
TOTAL COOKING TIME: 50 minutes
SERVES 4

1 tablespoon olive oil
1 large onion, chopped
2 cloves garlic, crushed
2 teaspoons sweet paprika
1 large potato, chopped
1 large carrot, sliced
400 g (14 oz) can chopped tomatoes
375 ml (1½ cups) vegetable stock
400 g (14 oz) orange sweet potato, cut
    into 1.5 cm (⅝ inch) cubes
150 g (5½ oz) broccoli, cut into florets
2 zucchini (courgettes), sliced
125 g (1 cup) self-raising flour
20 g (1 oz) chilled butter, cubed
2 teaspoons chopped fresh flat-leaf
    (Italian) parsley
1 teaspoon fresh thyme
1 teaspoon chopped fresh rosemary
80 ml (⅓ cup) milk
2 tablespoons sour cream

1 Heat the oil in a saucepan and add the onion. Cook over low heat, stirring occasionally, for 5 minutes, or until soft. Stir in the garlic and paprika and cook, stirring, for 1 minute.

2 Add the potato, carrot, tomato and stock to the pan. Bring to the boil, then reduce the heat and simmer, covered, for 10 minutes. Add the sweet potato, broccoli and zucchini and simmer for 10 minutes, or until tender. Preheat the oven to moderately hot 200°C (400°F/Gas 6).

3 Sift the flour and a pinch of salt into a bowl and add the butter. Rub the butter into the flour with your fingertips until it resembles fine breadcrumbs. Stir in the herbs and make a well in the centre. Add the milk, and mix with a flat-bladed knife, using a cutting action, until the mixture comes together in beads. Gather up the dough and lift onto a lightly floured surface. Divide into eight portions, shaping each into a ball.

4 Add the sour cream to the casserole. Transfer to a 2 litre (8 cup) ovenproof dish and top with the dumplings. Bake for 20 minutes, or until golden and a skewer comes out clean.

Cook all the vegetables until they are tender.

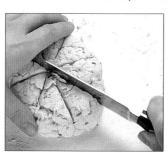

Divide the dough into eight equal portions.

Eggplant and Spinach Terrine

PREPARATION TIME: 1 hour +
overnight refrigeration
TOTAL COOKING TIME: 55 minutes
SERVES 6

3 large red capsicums (peppers)
1 large old potato, halved
40 g (1½ oz) butter
2 cloves garlic, crushed
800 g (1 lb 12 oz) English spinach leaves,
  shredded
60 ml (¼ cup) cream
1 egg yolk
80 ml (⅓ cup) olive oil
2 eggplants (aubergines), cut into thin slices
  lengthways
30 g (1 cup) fresh basil
350 g (12 oz) ricotta
2 cloves garlic, crushed, extra

1 Cut capsicums into large pieces,
removing seeds and membranes.
Cook, skin-side-up, under a hot grill
(broiler) until skin blisters. Peel.

2 Preheat the oven to moderate 180°C (350°F/Gas 4).
Grease and line a 1.5 litre (6 cup) terrine. Bring a
saucepan of salted water to the boil and cook the
potato for 10 minutes. Drain, cool. Cut into thin
slices.

3 Melt butter in a large saucepan and cook garlic for
30 seconds. Add spinach and toss. Steam, covered,
over low heat for 2–3 minutes, or until wilted. Cool
slightly and place in a food processor or blender
and process until smooth. Squeeze out any excess
liquid, place in a bowl and stir in cream and egg.

4 Heat a chargrill plate or griddle over high heat and
brush with some of the oil. Cook the eggplant for
2–3 minutes each side, or until golden, brushing
with the remaining oil.

5 To assemble, arrange one third of eggplant neatly
in base of the terrine, cutting to fit. Top with a
layer of half the capsicum, spinach mixture, basil,
all the potato, and all the combined ricotta and
garlic. Repeat with remaining ingredients, finishing
with eggplant. Oil a piece of foil and cover terrine,
sealing well. Place in a baking dish and half fill
with water. Bake for 25–30
minutes. Remove from oven,
put a piece of cardboard on
top and weigh it down with
small food cans. Chill
overnight.

6 Turn out and cut into slices.

*Blend the spinach mixture in a
food processor until smooth.*

*Spread a layer of spinach mixture
over second layer of capsicum.*

Ratatouille Tarte Tatin

PREPARATION TIME: 45 minutes +
20 minutes refrigeration
TOTAL COOKING TIME: 50 minutes
SERVES 6

185 g (1½ cups) plain (all-purpose) flour
90 g (3¼ oz) butter, chopped
1 egg
1 tablespoon oil
20 g (¾ oz) butter, extra
2 zucchini (courgettes), halved lengthways
　and sliced
250 g (9 oz) eggplant (aubergines), cut into
　2 cm (¾ inch) cubes
1 red capsicum (pepper), cut into 2 cm
　(¾ inch) cubes
1 green capsicum (pepper), cut into 2 cm
　(¾ inch) cubes
1 large red onion, cut into 2 cm (¾ inch)
　cubes
250 g (9 oz) cherry tomatoes, halved
2 tablespoons balsamic vinegar
60 g (½ cup) grated Cheddar
300 g (10½ oz) sour cream
60 g (¼ cup) good-quality pesto

1 Sift the flour into a bowl. Add the butter and rub into the flour with your fingertips until it resembles fine breadcrumbs. Make a well in the centre, add the egg (and 2 tablespoons water if it is too dry) and mix with a flat-bladed knife, using a cutting action, until it comes together in beads. Gather the dough together and lift onto a floured work surface. Press into a ball, flatten slightly into a disc, wrap in plastic wrap and chill for 20 minutes.

2 Preheat the oven to moderately hot 200°C (400°F/Gas 6). Grease and line a 25 cm (10 inch) springform tin. Heat the oil and extra butter in a frying pan and cook the zucchini, eggplant, capsicums and onion over high heat for 8 minutes, or until just soft. Add the tomatoes and vinegar and cook for 3–4 minutes.

3 Place the tin on a baking tray and neatly lay the vegetables in the tin, then sprinkle with cheese. Roll the dough out between two sheets of baking paper to a 28 cm (11 inch) circle. Remove the paper and invert the pastry into the tin over the filling. Tuck the edges of the pastry down the side of the tin. Bake for 30–35 minutes (some liquid will leak out), then stand for 1–2 minutes. Invert onto a platter. Combine the sour cream and pesto. Serve with the tarte tatin.

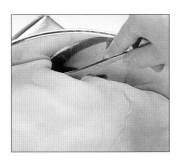

Add cherry tomatoes and vinegar and cook for 3–4 minutes.

Use a spoon handle to tuck edges of pastry down the side of tin.

Spinach Pie

PREPARATION TIME: 45 minutes +
1 hour refrigeration
TOTAL COOKING TIME: 55 minutes
SERVES 6

Pastry
250 g (2 cups) plain (all-purpose) flour
30 g (1 oz) chilled butter, chopped
60 ml (¼ cup) olive oil

Filling
500 g (1 lb 2 oz) English spinach leaves
2 teaspoons olive oil
1 onion, finely chopped
3 spring onions (scallions), finely chopped
200 g (7 oz) feta, crumbled
2 tablespoons chopped fresh flat-leaf
   (Italian) parsley
1 tablespoon chopped fresh dill
2 tablespoons grated kefalotyri cheese
45 g (¼ cup) cooked white rice
40 g (¼ cup) pine nuts, toasted and roughly
   chopped
¼ teaspoon ground nutmeg
½ teaspoon ground cumin
3 eggs, lightly beaten

1 Lightly grease a shallow 17 x 26 cm
(6¾ x 10½ inch) tin. To make the
pastry, sift the flour and ½ teaspoon
salt into a bowl. Add the butter and
rub in with your fingertips until the
mixture resembles fine breadcrumbs. Make a well in the centre
and add the oil. Using your hands,

mix together. Add 125 ml (½ cup) warm water and
mix with a flat-bladed knife, using a cutting action
until the mixture comes together in beads. Gently
gather the dough together and lift out onto a
lightly floured surface. Press into a ball and flatten
into a disc. Wrap in plastic wrap and refrigerate
for 1 hour.

2 Trim and wash the spinach, then coarsely chop.
Wrap in a tea towel and squeeze out excess mois-
ture. Heat the oil in a frying pan, add the onion
and spring onion and cook over low heat, without
browning, for 5 minutes, or until softened. Place
in a bowl with the spinach and the remaining
filling ingredients and mix well. Season.

3 Preheat the oven to moderately hot 200°C
(400°F/Gas 6). Roll out half the pastry between
two sheets of baking paper, remove the top sheet
and invert the pastry into the tin, allowing any
excess to hang over the sides. Spoon the filling
into the tin. Roll out the remaining pastry large
enough to cover the top. Place over the filling and
press the pastry edges firmly to seal. Trim away
any extra pastry. Brush the top with a little oil,
then score three strips lengthways, then on the
diagonal to make a diamond pattern on the
surface. Make two slits in the top to allow steam
to escape.

4 Bake for 45–50 minutes, covering with foil if the
surface becomes too brown. The pie is cooked
when it slides when the tin is gently shaken. Turn
out onto a rack for 10 minutes, then cut into
pieces and serve.

All our recipes are thoroughly tested in a specially developed test kitchen. Standard metric measuring cups and spoons are used in the development of our recipes. All cup and spoon measurements are level. We have used 60 g (2¼ oz/Grade 3) eggs in all recipes. Sizes of cans vary from manufacturer to manufacturer and between countries – use the can size closest to the one suggested in the recipe.

CONVERSION GUIDE

1 cup = 250 ml (9 fl oz)

1 teaspoon = 5 ml

1 Australian tablespoon = 20 ml (4 teaspoons)

1 UK/US tablespoon = 15 ml (3 teaspoons)

Where temperature ranges are indicated, the lower figure applies to gas ovens, the higher to electric ovens. This allows for the fact that the flame in gas ovens generates a drier heat, which effectively cooks food faster than the moister heat of an electric oven, even if the temperature setting is the same.

DRY MEASURES	LIQUID MEASURES	LINEAR MEASURES
30 g = 1 oz	30 ml = 1 fl oz	6 mm = ¼ inch
250 g = 9 oz	125 ml = 4 fl oz	1 cm = ½ inch
500 g = 1 lb 2 oz	250 ml = 9 fl oz	2.5 cm = 1 inch

	°C	°F	GAS MARK
Very slow	120	250	½
Slow	150	300	2
Mod slow	160	325	3
Moderate	180	350	4
Mod hot	190(g)–210(e)	375–425	5
Hot	200(g)–240(e)	400–475	6
Very hot	230(g)–260(e)	450–525	8

CUP CONVERSIONS – DRY INGREDIENTS

1 cup almonds, slivered whole = 125 g (4½ oz)

1 cup cheese, lightly packed processed cheddar = 155 g (5½oz)

1 cup wheat flour = 125 g (4½ oz)

1 cup wholemeal flour = 140 g (5 oz)

1 cup minced (ground) meat = 250 g (9 oz)

1 cup pasta shapes = 125 g (4½ oz)

1 cup raisins = 170 g (6 oz)

1 cup rice, short grain, raw = 200 g (7 oz)

1 cup sesame seeds = 160 g (6 oz)

1 cup split peas = 250 g (9 oz)

(g) = gas (e) = electric

Note: For fan-forced ovens, check your appliance manual, but as a general rule, set the oven temperature to 20°C lower than the temperature indicated in the recipe.

INTERNATIONAL GLOSSARY

capsicum	sweet bell pepper	cornflour	cornstarch
chick pea	garbanzo bean	eggplant	aubergine
chilli	chile, chili pepper	spring onion	scallion
		zucchini	courgette

First published in 2004 by Murdoch Books Pty Limited.
Erico House, 6th Floor North, 93-99 Upper Richmond Road, Putney, London, SW15 2TG, United Kingdom.

This edition published in 2006 for Index Books Ltd, Garrard Way, Kettering, NN16 8TD, United Kingdom.

ISBN 1 74045 953 9
Printed by Sing Cheong Printing Co. Ltd. PRINTED IN CHINA.